CONTENTS

Helping or HURTING?

Adults and kids around the world enjoy playing many different sports. Playing sports is good exercise and can help people stay fit and healthy. Sometimes, though, playing sports can cause people to become hurt, or injured. In some cases, these injuries can be very **serious**.

Some people worry that certain sports are too dangerous, or unsafe, for kids to play. Other people believe all sports help much more than they hurt. These different points of view often play a part in what sports kids are allowed to play.

Know the Facts!

As of 2016, 37 percent of children in the United States played **organized** team sports.

POINTS OF VIEW

Are Some SPORTS Too Dangerous for Kids?

By Amy B. Rogers

KidHaven PUBLISHING

Published in 2019 by
KidHaven Publishing, an Imprint of Greenhaven Publishing, LLC
353 3rd Avenue
Suite 255
New York, NY 10010

Designer: Deanna Paternostro
Editor: Katie Kawa

Photo credits: Cover SUSAN LEGGETT/Shutterstock.com; pp. 5, 17, 21 (inset, right) Steve Debenport/E+/Getty Images; p. 7 Icon Sportswire/Contributor/Icon Sportswire/Getty Images; p. 9 Hero Images/Hero Images/Getty Images; p. 11 Jeff Thrower/Shutterstock.com; p. 13 (top left) Lucky Business/Shutterstock.com; p. 13 (top right) Monkey Business Images/Shutterstock.com; p. 13 (bottom left) Jon Osumi/Shutterstock.com; p. 13 (bottom right) Suzanne Tucker/Shutterstock.com; pp. 15, 19 (bottom) Fotokostic/Shutterstock.com; p. 19 (top) Sergey Maksienko/Shutterstock.com; p. 21 (notepad) ESB Professional/Shutterstock.com; p. 21 (markers) Kucher Serhii/Shutterstock.com; p. 21 (photo frame) FARBAI/iStock/Thinkstock; p. 21 (inset, left) tammykayphoto/Shutterstock.com; p. 21 (inset, middle-left) Jarva Jar/Shutterstock.com; p. 21 (inset, middle-right) Wendy Nero/Shutterstock.com.

Cataloging-in-Publication Data

Names: Rogers, Amy B.
Title: Are some sports too dangerous for kids? / Amy B. Rogers.
Description: New York : KidHaven Publishing, 2019. | Series: Points of view | Includes glossary and index.
Identifiers: ISBN 9781534525603 (pbk.) | 9781534525597 (library bound) | ISBN 9781534525610 (6 pack) | ISBN 9781534525627 (ebook)
Subjects: LCSH: Sports–Social aspects–Juvenile literature. | Sports for children–Juvenile literature.
Classification: LCC GV706.5 R638 2019 | DDC 796.083–dc23

Printed in the United States of America

CPSIA compliance information: Batch #BS18KL: For further information contact Greenhaven Publishing LLC, New York, New York at 1-844-317-7404.

Please visit our website, www.greenhavenpublishing.com. For a free color catalog of all our high-quality books, call toll free 1-844-317-7404 or fax 1-844-317-7405.

It's good to have an informed, or educated, opinion about issues such as the dangers of sports. Learning all the facts about an issue is how you **develop** an informed opinion.

The Dangers of CONCUSSIONS

Sports safety for both children and adults is in the news often. This is mainly because new studies have been done that show how serious certain sports injuries are.

One of these serious injuries is a concussion, or a brain injury caused by a bump or hit to the head. It can also be caused by a hit to another part of the body that makes the brain move around in the **skull**. Concussions can continue to cause problems such as memory loss and mood changes many years after they first happen.

Know the Facts!

Football has the highest concussion rate and number of total injuries for youth sports.

Today, **athletes**, coaches, and other adults are more aware of the dangers of concussions than they were years ago. They know certain sports, such as football and cheerleading, put athletes at a greater **risk** for getting a concussion than other sports.

Concussions and Collision SPORTS

Many people are afraid of how a concussion can **affect** the brain of a child whose body is still developing. To **protect** children from concussions, some people believe they shouldn't be allowed to play collision sports, or sports that feature one player hitting another with great force, such as football or ice hockey.

Other people believe children can still play these sports if the rules are changed to make them less dangerous. They believe taking tackling out of youth football and body checking out of youth hockey will make them safer.

Know the Facts!

A major study of youth sports injuries was done in 2012. That year, 163,670 children went to the **emergency room** with a concussion.

Girls report getting concussions while playing sports more often than boys do.

Staying SAFE

Some people believe the only way to stop kids from getting concussions while playing sports is to keep them from playing sports that cause them. However, other people believe these sports aren't too dangerous. They believe they're safer than ever before because of changes to the rules to better protect players.

In some cases, the gear players wear has also changed to make sports safer. Better helmets, pads, masks, and mouth guards help protect players from injuries. Also, better methods of training for players, coaches, and doctors are being used to keep young athletes safe.

Know the Facts!

Many concussions during soccer games happen when players head the ball, or hit it with their head. Because of this, U.S. Soccer has stated that no child under 10 years old should be allowed to head the ball.

It's important to always wear the proper safety equipment, or gear, when playing sports.

Contact Causes INJURY

Concussions aren't the only reason some people believe certain sports aren't safe for kids. There are many other injuries that can occur while playing sports that can send a child to the hospital, require **surgery**, or cause an athlete a lot of pain. These injuries include breaks, sprains, and tears to bones and muscles.

A 2017 study stated that many of these injuries wouldn't happen if collision and contact sports no longer featured players hitting each other. In contact sports, players often hit or bump into each other, but they do so with less force than in collision sports.

Know the Facts!

Sports injuries make up more than 30 percent of all the injuries children get each year.

collision sport

contact sport

Limited-contact sports don't often have contact between players, and noncontact sports keep players separate from each other. **Experts** believe these sports are much safer than collision and contact sports.

limited-contact sport

noncontact sport

What's the RISK?

Collision and contact sports cause the highest number of injuries for kids, but they're not the only sports that can be dangerous. All sports and **physical** activities present some risk of injury. However, organized sports—even collision sports—have rules in place and adults watching to keep kids as safe as possible.

Many doctors also report that the risk of injury for young athletes is still fairly low. Around 30 million kids play organized sports each year in the United States, but only around 3.5 million of these young athletes get injured.

Know the Facts!

More than 1 million kids play organized football in the United States.

Many people believe sports are a safe way for kids to spend time being active with friends.

Lifelong PROBLEMS

Sports often give kids good memories that they carry with them throughout their lives. However, they sometimes give kids health problems that they carry with them throughout their lives, too. Collision and contact sports can cause injuries such as broken bones that lead to chronic, or long-lasting, pain.

Brain injuries have become the biggest concern people have about the long-term effects of sports. Concussions can lead to a serious brain disease known as CTE that causes many problems, such as memory loss and anger issues. Doctors have found that CTE can happen even in people who stopped playing sports after high school.

Know the Facts!

Scientists have found that football players who began playing the sport before they were 12 years old had a higher risk of problems with their brain development than athletes who began playing later.

Concussions and other sports injuries can have serious long-term effects on a person's life. Some people believe playing a sport isn't worth the future health problems sports can cause.

A Different Kind of DANGER

Although athletes sometimes deal with serious health problems, many experts say possible dangers are no reason to stay away from playing all sports. Instead, they say the health benefits of sports generally are greater than many of the risks.

Exercise is one important way to fight childhood obesity, which is the state of being very overweight. Obesity can cause many health problems, so it's important for kids to stay active. Playing sports is a good way for kids to stay healthy and fit. It's also a way for kids to make friends and learn to feel good about themselves.

Know the Facts!

Studies have shown that students who are physically active, such as students who play sports, generally have better grades than students who aren't active.

Many people believe not being active at all is much more dangerous than playing sports.

What's Best for KIDS?

Many people love sports such as football and hockey. They believe the benefits of these sports are much more important than any possible dangers. They also believe these sports are becoming even safer because of better equipment and training.

However, another group of people believes these sports cause too many serious injuries. They believe they're protecting kids by trying to keep them from playing sports they see as too dangerous. Both groups of people want to do the right thing for young athletes, but they have different ideas about what's best.

Know the Facts!

The U.S. Department of Health and Human Services, which is a part of the government that works to protect the health of Americans, has stated that children should get at least one hour of physical activity every day.

Are some sports too dangerous for kids?

YES

- Some sports have a much higher risk of concussions than other sports.
- Collision and contact sports cause many serious injuries.
- Some sports can cause long-term health problems.

NO

- Better equipment, rules, and training are helping protect against concussions and other injuries.
- The injury risk in youth sports is still fairly low.
- Sports are more helpful than harmful for a person's health because they keep people active.

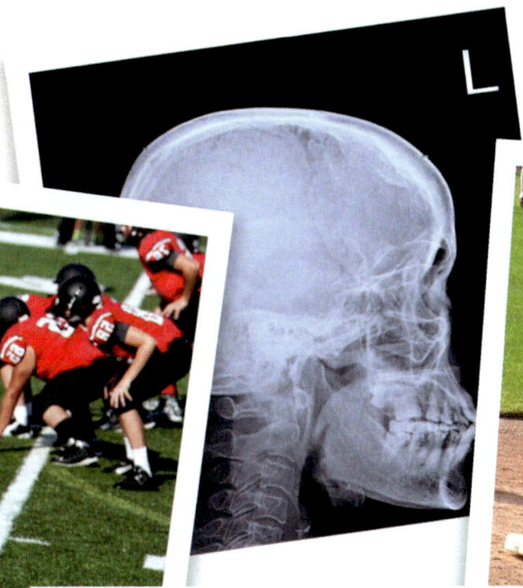

Do you think some sports are too dangerous for kids? How did learning the facts about sports injuries and the benefits of sports help you form your point of view?

GLOSSARY

affect: To produce an effect on something.

athlete: A person who plays a sport.

develop: To create over time. Also, to cause to grow bigger or more advanced.

emergency room: A part of a hospital used to treat people who need immediate medical care.

expert: Someone who has a special skill or knowledge.

organized: Put together in a formal way with leaders and rules for doing things.

physical: Relating to the body.

protect: To keep safe.

risk: The possibility that something bad will happen.

serious: Causing worry or harm.

skull: The bones that form the head and face of a person or animal.

surgery: A medical treatment that involves cutting into the body.

For More INFORMATION

WEBSITES

Exercise and Sports Safety
kidshealth.org/en/kids/nutrition/sports-safety
This part of the KidsHealth website directs visitors to pages that address many different areas of sports safety, including concussions and other injuries.

Sports and Your Eyes
nei.nih.gov/kids/sports_and_your_eyes
This website presents different sports and how much of a danger they are to a person's eyes, as well as facts about keeping your eyes safe while playing sports.

BOOKS

Hudson, Maryann. *Concussions in Sports*. Minneapolis, MN: ABDO Publishing Company, 2014.

Lang, Elizabeth. *Sports Safety*. Mankato, MN: Child's World, 2014.

Nagelhout, Ryan. *What if I Get a Concussion?* New York, NY: Gareth Stevens Publishing, 2017.

Publisher's note to educators and parents: Our editors have carefully reviewed these websites to ensure that they are suitable for students. Many websites change frequently, however, and we cannot guarantee that a site's future contents will continue to meet our high standards of quality and educational value. Be advised that students should be closely supervised whenever they access the Internet.

INDEX